I0426014

May 2012

STREAMLINING GOVERNMENT

Questions to Consider When Evaluating Proposals to Consolidate Physical Infrastructure and Management Functions

G A O
Accountability ★ Integrity ★ Reliability

GAO-12-542

May 2012

STREAMLINING GOVERNMENT

Questions to Consider When Evaluating Proposals to Consolidate Physical Infrastructure and Management Functions

Why GAO Did This Study

GAO has previously reported on many areas that appear to be duplicative, overlapping, or fragmented and has suggested that agencies could increase their efficiency and effectiveness by consolidating their physical infrastructure, such as research facilities, or consolidating their management functions, such as information technology. Such consolidation, however, involves weighing costs as well as benefits and can be complex and challenging to implement.

Given the potential benefits and costs of consolidation, it is imperative that Congress and the executive branch have the information needed to help effectively evaluate consolidation proposals. In this report, GAO identifies key questions that agencies should consider when evaluating whether to consolidate physical infrastructure and management functions and illustrates the questions with agency consolidation examples. GAO reviewed the consolidation literature; selected seven consolidation initiatives at the federal level in various stages of completion and one recommended consolidation; reviewed documentation and interviewed agency officials with responsibility for the initiatives; and interviewed public-management and government-reform experts with consolidation experience. GAO provided the draft for review and comment to the five agencies with consolidation initiatives that were not covered by prior GAO work and made technical changes as appropriate. GAO does not make recommendations in this report.

View GAO-12-542. For more information, contact J. Christopher Mihm at (202) 512-6806 or mihmj@gao.gov.

What GAO Found

The following fundamental questions should be answered while considering a physical infrastructure or management function consolidation initiative.

Key Questions to Consider When Evaluating Consolidation Proposals

What are the goals of the consolidation? What opportunities will be addressed through the consolidation and what problems will be solved? What problems, if any, will be created?
What will be the likely costs and benefits of the consolidation? Are sufficiently reliable data available to support a business-case analysis or cost-benefit analysis?
How can the up-front costs associated with the consolidation be funded?
Who are the consolidation stakeholders, and how will they be affected? How have the stakeholders been involved in the decision, and how have their views been considered? On balance, do stakeholders understand the rationale for consolidation?
To what extent do plans show that change management practices will be used to implement the consolidation?

Source: GAO.

- The key to any consolidation initiative is the identification of and agreement on specific goals, with the consolidation goals being evaluated against a realistic expectation of how they can be achieved. Consolidation goals, for example, can be compromised and new problems introduced when an initiative is delayed or halted, with agencies running the risk of increased costs.

- The initiative needs to be based on a clearly presented business-case or cost-benefit analysis and grounded in accurate and reliable data, both of which can show stakeholders why a particular initiative is being considered and the range of alternatives considered.

- Physical infrastructure and management function consolidations often have up-front costs, such as paying for equipment and furniture moves and funding employee transfers, and agencies find it challenging to pay for these upfront costs.

- Since stakeholders often view consolidation as working against their own interests, it is critical that agencies identify who the relevant stakeholders are and develop a two-way communication strategy that both addresses their concerns and conveys the rationale for and overarching benefits associated with the consolidation.

- Finally, implementing a large-scale organizational transformation, such as a consolidation, requires the concentrated efforts of both leadership and employees to accomplish new organizational goals. Agencies should have an implementation plan for the consolidation that includes essential change management practices such as active, engaged leadership of executives at the highest possible levels; a dedicated implementation team that can be held accountable for change; and a strategy for capturing best practices, measuring progress toward the established goals of the consolidation, retaining key talent, and assessing and mitigating risk, among others.

Contents

Abbreviations

BRAC	Base Realignment and Closure
COBRA	Cost of Base Realignment Actions
DOD	Department of Defense
EPA	Environmental Protection Agency
FDCCI	Federal Data Center Consolidation Initiative
FHCC	Federal Health Care Center
HUD	Department of Housing and Urban Development
ICASS	International Cooperative Administrative Support Services
IRS	Internal Revenue Service
OMB	Office of Management and Budget
OPM	Office of Personnel Management
State	Department of State
TIGTA	Treasury Inspector General for Tax Administration
USAID	U.S. Agency for International Development
VA	Department of Veterans Affairs

United States Government Accountability Office
Washington, DC 20548

May 23, 2012

The Honorable Daniel K. Akaka
Chairman
Subcommittee on Oversight of Government Management, the Federal
   Workforce, and the District of Columbia
Committee on Homeland Security and Governmental Affairs
United States Senate

The Honorable Thomas R. Carper
Chairman
Subcommittee on Federal Financial Management, Government
   Information, Federal Services, and International Security
Committee on Homeland Security and Governmental Affairs
United States Senate

The Honorable Mark R. Warner
Chairman
Task Force on Government Performance
Committee on the Budget
United States Senate

The current fiscal crisis offers a window of opportunity for the federal
government to examine how consolidating its operations can contribute to
cost savings or effectiveness gains. With our nation facing serious, long-
term fiscal challenges, a reevaluation of federal agencies' operations has
never been more important than it is today, and over the past 2 years, we
have reported on many areas that appear to be duplicative, overlapping,
or fragmented. The first report, issued in March 2011, presented 81
opportunities to reduce potential government duplication, achieve cost
savings, or enhance revenues, and the 2012 report presented 51 areas
where programs may be able to achieve greater efficiencies or become
more effective in providing government services. For example, the Army
and Navy are planning to spend approximately $1.6 billion to acquire
separate unmanned aircraft systems that are likely to have similar
capabilities. In addition, landholding agencies have over 45,000
underused buildings, and individual agencies have hundreds of
incompatible information-technology networks and systems that were built
over time and hinder governmentwide information sharing. This

duplication of effort and the maintenance of these buildings and legacy systems are costly propositions for the federal government.[1]

In our past reports, we have suggested that federal agencies could increase their efficiency and effectiveness by consolidating their physical infrastructure, such as closing offices or other facilities like military bases, storage depots, and research facilities, or consolidating their management functions, such as information-technology or administrative-support services.[2] At your request, in this report we are examining key questions to consider when evaluating physical infrastructure and management function consolidation initiatives, with physical infrastructure consolidation defined as the combining of systems, equipment, and people into fewer buildings or facilities than they previously occupied and management function consolidation as the combining of formerly distinct systems, processes, and people in areas such as information technology, financial management, human resources management, and procurement. Both types of consolidation are intended to support improved customer service, increased efficiency and effectiveness, or cost avoidances and cost savings, or a mix of those goals.

Consolidation is beneficial in some situations and not in others, and so a case-by-case analysis is necessary, evaluating the goals of the consolidation against the realistic possibility of the extent to which those goals would be achieved. Consolidation initiatives can be immensely complex, politically charged, and costly and are not quick, easy, or automatic ways of producing desired change. Decision makers need to balance the benefits of consolidation against the physical, up-front financial, bureaucratic, and political costs, while considering alternatives such as increased cooperation or collaboration that may provide other

---

[1]GAO, *2012 Annual Report: Opportunities to Reduce Duplication, Overlap and Fragmentation, Achieve Savings, and Enhance Revenue*, GAO-12-342SP (Washington, D.C.: Feb. 28, 2012) and *Opportunities to Reduce Potential Duplication in Government Programs, Save Tax Dollars, and Enhance Revenue*, GAO-11-318SP (Washington, D.C.: Mar. 1, 2011).

[2]See, for example, GAO, *Opportunities for Oversight and Improved Use of Taxpayer Funds*, GAO-03-1006 (Washington, D.C.: Aug. 1, 2003); *Best Practices: Elements Critical to Successfully Reducing Unneeded RDT&E Infrastructure*, GAO/NSIAD/RCED-98-23 (Washington, D.C.: Jan. 8, 1998); and *Embassy Management: Actions Are Needed to Increase Efficiency and Improve Delivery of Administrative Support Services*, GAO-04-511 (Washington, D.C.: Sept. 7, 2004).

GAO-12-542 Consolidation Proposals

paths to efficiency.[3] In addition, consolidation initiatives may, but do not inevitably, save money and often require significant up-front costs to yield long-term benefits. There are, however, situations with clear potential for cost savings and operational efficiencies through physical infrastructure and management function consolidations.

Given the potential benefits and challenges of consolidation, it is imperative that Congress and the executive branch have the tools and information needed to help effectively evaluate consolidation proposals and activities. In response to your request, the specific objective of this report was to identify key questions that federal agencies should consider when evaluating whether to consolidate physical infrastructure or management functions and illustrate the questions with agency consolidation examples. To address this objective, we identified and reviewed our reports on specific consolidation initiatives that have been undertaken.[4] We used this to complement information gathered through a review of the relevant literature on public-sector consolidations produced by academic institutions, professional associations, think tanks, news outlets, and various other organizations. In addition, as illustrative examples, we reviewed selected consolidation initiatives at the federal agency level. These examples provided insights into how agencies addressed the key questions. The examples were selected from physical infrastructure and management function consolidations from a range of agencies in different stages of completion, including one that has been recommended but not acted upon. The examples represented both inter- and intra-agency activity. We obtained documentation on these initiatives and interviewed agency officials with responsibility for implementing the initiatives. We did not verify the estimated cost savings associated with the consolidation initiatives. Table 1 provides a description of the illustrative examples we included in the report. We also interviewed a

---

[3]See, for example, GAO, *Results-Oriented Government: Practices That Can Help Enhance and Sustain Collaboration among Federal Agencies,* GAO-06-15 (Washington, D.C.: Oct. 21, 2005). We are also in the process of assessing interagency collaboration mechanisms with a report scheduled for release in fall 2012.

[4]See, for example, GAO, *Data Center Consolidation: Agencies Need to Complete Inventories and Plans to Achieve Expected Savings,* GAO-11-565 (Washington, D.C.: July 19, 2011); *Embassy Management: State Department and Other Agencies Should Further Explore Opportunities to Save Administrative Costs Overseas,* GAO-12-317 (Washington, D.C.: Jan 31, 2012); and *Military Bases: Analysis of DOD's 2005 Selection Process and Recommendations for Base Closures and Realignments,* GAO-05-785 (Washington, D.C.: July 1, 2005).

number of individuals selected for their expertise in public management and government reform. We conducted some of these interviews individually and met with a panel of Fellows from the National Academy of Public Administration, where participants shared their thoughts on the basis of their consolidation experiences.[5]

Table 1: Descriptions of a Recommended Federal Agency Consolidation and Other Consolidation Initiatives in Various Stages of Implementation

Consolidation initiative	Type of consolidation	Description
Department of Commerce Census Bureau Regional Offices	Intra-agency / physical infrastructure	The Census Bureau in 2011 announced plans to close 6 out of 12 regional offices by 2013 to reduce the cost and improve the quality of the hundreds of surveys the Census Bureau conducts annually. The Census Bureau estimates the initiative will save between $15 million and $18 million annually beginning in fiscal year 2014.
Department of Defense (DOD) Base Realignment and Closure (BRAC)	Intra-agency / physical infrastructure	BRAC recommendations are intended to generate savings, reduce excess property, and realign DOD's workload and workforce to achieve efficiencies through consolidating bases and military functions. The BRAC 2005 round, the fifth such round undertaken by DOD since 1988, is the biggest, most complex, and costliest BRAC round to date. DOD reported that as a result of prior BRAC rounds, billions of dollars had been saved annually that could be applied to higher priority defense needs.
Department of the Treasury Internal Revenue Service (IRS) Processing Centers	Intra-agency / physical infrastructure	Beginning in 2000, IRS consolidated the total number of individual paper processing centers from eight to three sites to reduce overhead and real-estate costs and improve efficiency in response to the increase in electronic filing and subsequent decrease in paper filing. IRS estimates the initiative has saved $175 million through 2011.
Environmental Protection Agency (EPA) Laboratories	Recommended intra-agency / physical infrastructure	Multiple independent evaluations over the past 20 years have recommended that EPA address planning, coordination, and leadership issues associated with EPA's science activities. EPA has also not fully addressed recommendations from a 1994 independent evaluation to consolidate and realign its laboratory facilities and workforce—even though this evaluation found that the geographic separation of laboratories hampered their efficiency and technical operations and that consolidation and realignment could improve planning and coordination issues that have disadvantaged its science and technical community for decades.

---

[5]Established in 1967 and chartered by Congress, the National Academy of Public Administration is a non-profit, independent coalition of public management and organizational leaders. For more information, go to www.napawash.org.

Consolidation initiative	Type of consolidation	Description
Office of Management and Budget (OMB) Federal Data Center Consolidation Initiative (FDCCI)	Intra-agency / physical infrastructure and management function	The FDCCI is intended to improve the efficiency, performance, and environmental footprint of federal data center activities through the consolidation of centers that support data transmissions. The initiative was announced in 2010 and is planned to continue through 2015. OMB estimated that the federal government will save approximately $3 billion between 2011 and 2015.
Office of Personnel Management (OPM) Payroll Systems	Interagency / management function	The payroll consolidation initiative consolidated 26 payroll systems to four shared-service centers, standardized payroll policies and procedures, and simplified and better integrated payroll, human resources, and finance functions between its announcement in 2001 and its completion in 2009. OPM estimated the initiative would save the federal government $1.1 billion over 10 years.
Department of State (State) International Cooperative Administrative Support Services (ICASS) system	Interagency / management function	ICASS is an interagency system established in 1997 for distributing the costs of administrative services at overseas posts and is intended to ensure that each agency bears the cost of its overseas presence. State has the primary responsibility for operating the system, and over 40 agencies share the costs of ICASS services, which totaled over $2 billion in fiscal year 2011. State estimated that the U.S. government saved millions of dollars per year by reducing staff and eliminating warehouses. However, there has been no quantitative study on cost savings because the necessary data are not available.
Department of Veterans Affairs (VA) and DOD Federal Health Care Center (FHCC)	Interagency / physical infrastructure and management function	The FHCC is an ongoing 5-year demonstration project running from 2010 to 2015 to integrate VA and DOD medical care into a first-of-its-kind joint facility that will provide health care services to approximately 118,000 VA and DOD patients per year. VA and DOD officials estimated that the first two phases of the initiative saved $11.2 million.

Source: GAO.

We conducted our work from June 2011 to May 2012 in accordance with all sections of GAO's Quality Assurance Framework that are relevant to our objective. The framework requires that we plan and perform the engagement to obtain sufficient and appropriate evidence to meet our stated objectives and to discuss any limitations in our work. We believe that the information and data obtained, and the analysis conducted, provide a reasonable basis for any findings and conclusions in this report. More detailed information on our scope and methodology appears in appendix I.

Background

Physical infrastructure and management function consolidations can be strategies to help improve the efficiency of federal agencies, an area with increased focus given our current fiscal challenges. In the 2013 budget, for example, the administration reported that it is proposing cuts, consolidations, and savings across the government totaling more than $24 billion in the upcoming fiscal year and $520 billion through 2022.[6] The White House also posted an interactive map of excess federal properties on its website, noting that the map illustrates a sampling of over 7,000 buildings and structures designated as excess. To help address this problem, an executive order, signed by the President in February 2004, promotes efficient and economical use of the federal government's real property assets by requiring each agency to determine what it owns, what it needs, and what it costs to manage its real properties. The agencies then are required to develop and implement asset-management plans, develop and monitor real-property performance measures, and dispose of properties that are not needed.[7] Another major approach that agencies can take to improve their cost effectiveness is to consolidate management or operational processes and functions to make them more efficient. This approach often involves examining administrative or operational processes to make them faster or to use fewer resources. While agency efficiency efforts will not resolve the long-term fiscal imbalance because of the size of that imbalance, they remain important to the federal government's ability to operate with fewer resources while maintaining or improving the critical services and functions that it provides.

A recent effort underway to address the need for reexamining government is the consideration of the Reforming and Consolidating Government Act of 2012 (S. 2129), first proposed by the President and introduced in the Senate by Senators Lieberman and Warner.[8] Under S. 2129, the President would be permitted to propose the creation of a new department (or renaming of an existing department), the abolishment or transfer of an executive department, or the consolidation of two or more

---

[6]Executive Office of the President of the United States, *Building a 21st Century Government by Cutting Duplication, Fragmentation, and Waste* (Washington, D.C.: Feb. 28, 2012).

[7]Exec. Order No. 13,327, Federal Real Property Asset Management, 69 Fed. Reg. 5897 (Feb. 4, 2004).

[8]S. 2129 112th Cong. (2012). On April 19, 2012, a companion bill was introduced in the House of Representatives, H.R. 4409 112th Cong. (2012).

GAO-12-542 Consolidation Proposals

departments.[9] However, it should be noted that none of the consolidation initiatives discussed in this report required this type of broad reorganization authority to be implemented, although some had specifically related legislation.

Key Questions to Consider When Evaluating Physical Infrastructure and Management Function Consolidation Proposals

The key questions we identified that federal agencies should consider when evaluating a physical infrastructure or management function consolidation initiative are presented in table 2.

Table 2: Key Questions to Consider When Evaluating Consolidation Proposals

What are the goals of the consolidation? What opportunities will be addressed through the consolidation and what problems will be solved? What problems, if any, will be created?
What will be the likely costs and benefits of the consolidation? Are sufficiently reliable data available to support a business-case analysis or cost-benefit analysis?
How can the up-front costs associated with the consolidation be funded?
Who are the consolidation stakeholders, and how will they be affected? How have the stakeholders been involved in the decision, and how have their views been considered? On balance, do stakeholders understand the rationale for consolidation?
To what extent do plans show that change management practices will be used to implement the consolidation?[a]

Source: GAO analysis.

[a]For these practices, we drew from our prior reports: *Highlights of a GAO Forum, Mergers and Transformation: Lessons Learned for a Department of Homeland Security and Other Federal Agencies*, GAO-03-293SP (Washington, D.C.: Nov. 14, 2002) and *Results-Oriented Cultures: Implementation Steps to Assist Mergers and Organizational Transformations*, GAO-03-669, (Washington, D.C.: July 23, 2003).

Appendix II has additional questions grouped by these five fundamental questions that are related to the ideas, strategies, and leading practices that may help facilitate physical infrastructure and management function consolidations.

[9]For our testimony on the legislation before the Senate Committee on Homeland Security and Governmental Affairs, see GAO, *Government Efficiency and Effectiveness: Opportunities for Improvement and Considerations for Restructuring*, GAO-12-454T (Washington, D.C.: Mar. 21, 2010).

What Are the Goals of the Consolidation? What Opportunities Will Be Addressed through the Consolidation and What Problems Will Be Solved? What Problems, If Any, Will Be Created?

We have previously reported and several experts we interviewed suggested that the key to any consolidation initiative is the identification of and agreement on specific goals, with the goals of the consolidation being evaluated against a realistic assessment of how the consolidation can achieve them. The process of defining goals can help decision makers reach a shared understanding of what problems genuinely need to be fixed, how to balance differing objectives, and what steps need to be taken to create not just short-term advantages but long-term gains.[10]

- For example, in 2000, Congress and IRS realized that some IRS paper processing site consolidation would be necessary to ensure efficient operations, while avoiding the expense of excess capacity. On the basis of the prior decreases in individual paper filings and the projected decreases that would become more dramatic in the future, IRS determined that it could process individual returns and satisfy customer needs at three sites, leading to the decision to close five other sites.[11]

- In fiscal year 2011, the Census Bureau decided to consolidate a field structure that had remained substantially unchanged for 50 years by closing 6 of 12 regional offices. The Census Bureau's overall goal for its regional office consolidation was creating a structure that would yield the highest quality data at the lowest possible cost. Census officials concluded that its current structure did not reflect advances in survey methodology and technology made in recent decades, such as the ability for home-based workers to have access to confidential data in full compliance with information technology security and legal restrictions. As a consequence, the bureau's method for conducting surveys was too costly, and survey sponsors, primarily other federal agencies, were demanding improved efficiency and increased responsiveness. Census established eight consolidation goals, shown in Table 3, each weighted by relative importance, and evaluated potential regional structures against these goals. According to Census officials, its consolidation will enable the bureau to save $15 million to

---

[10]GAO, *Executive Reorganization Authority: Balancing Executive and Congressional Roles in Shaping the Federal Government's Structure,* GAO-03-624T (Washington, D.C.: Apr. 3, 2003).

[11]Congress passed the Internal Revenue Service Restructuring and Reform Act of 1998, which established a performance goal of having 80 percent of individual tax returns e-filed by 2007, among other requirements. Pub. L. No. 105-206, 112 Stat. 685 (1998).

GAO-12-542 Consolidation Proposals

$18 million starting in fiscal year 2014 and improve the agency's ability to conduct surveys. The new design will also use improved management information systems and tools to maintain high-quality data collection.

Table 3: The Census Bureau's Eight Consolidation Goals

Goals
1. Minimize cost of survey operations
2. Improve data quality
3. Create a real-time information-rich management environment to enhance employee performance and management efficiencies
4. Create a more flexible management environment capable of adapting to changing conditions
5. Support multiple response modes more flexibly, involving the use of mailed paper questionnaires, Internet collection, computer-assisted telephone interviewing, and computer-assisted personal interviewing
6. Leverage local knowledge and facilitate outreach
7. Build a tested and reliable infrastructure upon which to scale up for the 2020 decennial census
8. Minimize vulnerability to natural disasters and unplanned events

Source: Census Bureau.

- In the late 1980s, changes in the national security environment resulted in a defense infrastructure with more bases than DOD needed. To address the problem of excess capacity and to realize cost savings, the Base Closure and Realignment Commission made a series of recommendations to close or consolidate DOD bases and military functions.[12] DOD has undergone five BRAC rounds beginning in 1988. Generally, the goals of the first four BRAC rounds were to generate savings to apply to other priorities, reduce property deemed excess to needs, and realign DOD's workload and workforce to achieve efficiencies in property management. As a result of prior BRAC rounds in 1988, 1991, 1993, and 1995, DOD reported that it

---

[12]The BRAC Commission for the 2005 round was a nine-member bipartisan commission, appointed by the President, which made recommendations on the basis of a review and analysis of recommendations from the Secretary of Defense, on base closures and realignments. The President and Congress had to accept or reject the commission's report in its entirety. National Defense Authorization Act for Fiscal Year 1990, Pub. L No. 101-510, title XXIX, Defense Base Closure and Realignment Act of 1990, 104 Stat. 1485, as amended by the National Defense Authorization Act for Fiscal Year 2002, Pub. L. No. 107-107, title XXX, 115 Stat. 1012, 1342-1353 (2001).

had reduced its domestic infrastructure, transferred hundreds of thousands of acres of unneeded property to other federal and nonfederal entities, and saved billions of dollars annually that could be applied to other higher priority defense needs.[13] For the BRAC 2005 round, the goals included transforming the military, fostering joint actions, and reducing excess infrastructure to produce savings. An example would be the BRAC recommendation to consolidate the supply, storage, and distribution function within the Defense Logistics Agency. As such, many of the BRAC 2005 recommendations involve complex realignments. Both DOD and the BRAC Commission reported that their primary consideration in making recommendations for the BRAC 2005 round was military value, which includes considerations such as an installation's current and future mission capabilities.[14]

- A central goal of the federal payroll consolidation initiative was achieving cost effectiveness through economies of scale and the elimination of duplicative systems. Other consolidation goals included standardizing payroll policies and procedures and simplifying and better integrating payroll, human resources, and finance functions. Cross-servicing and administrative consolidation initiatives began in the 1980s as part of the Reagan administration, and payroll was an early target of opportunity. In 2000, the Bush administration mandated e-government initiatives where common information technology solutions were identified. These were areas in which agencies historically had made significant individual investments to address needs that were common and duplicative. For example, OPM officials noted that many of the payroll systems were homegrown and on average about 20 years old, and many of the payroll service providers were considering capital investments in payroll-systems infrastructure. To avoid having individual agencies investing in new payroll systems, the administration selected 4 agency providers to serve as payroll providers in 2003; by 2009 these providers consolidated the payroll operations of the non-continuing agencies, absorbing their processing into existing systems. According to OPM officials, payroll consolidation was something that had been discussed for 30 years,

---

[13]GAO, *Federal Real Property: Progress Made on Planning and Data, but Unneeded Owned and Leased Facilities Remain*, GAO-11-520T (Washington, D.C.: Apr. 6, 2011).

[14]GAO, *Streamlining Government: Opportunities Exist to Strengthen OMB's Approach to Improving Efficiency*, GAO-10-394 (Washington, D.C.: May 7, 2010).

GAO-12-542 Consolidation Proposals

but the e-government mandate from the Bush administration finally gave OPM the power to make the consolidation happen.

Consolidation goals can be compromised and new problems introduced when an initiative is delayed, halted, or does not attract enough users to produce the economies of scale needed to generate cost savings. Under these fairly common conditions, participating agencies run the risk of seeing their costs increase.

- For example, State developed the ICASS system to streamline the provision of administrative services and cut costs for agencies located at overseas posts. However, we recently reported that many agencies continue to obtain services independently rather than through the ICASS system, which limits ICASS's ability to achieve greater economies of scale and deliver services efficiently.[15] To the extent that agencies do not participate in ICASS, and provide these services themselves, they are creating potentially duplicative administrative systems that may not be cost effective for the U.S. government as a whole. For example, we reported that several agencies procured their own appliances and shipped their own furniture rather than participate in the ICASS-managed collective pools. At one post, ICASS service providers had to remove and reinstall furniture at embassy-managed residences 67 times over a 6-month period as a result of agency officials being replaced in a home by officials from a different agency. Such additional work would not have been necessary if all agencies participated in the furniture and appliance pool.

---

[15]GAO-12-317.

What Will Be the Likely Costs and Benefits of the Consolidation? Are Sufficiently Reliable Data Available to Support a Business-Case Analysis or Cost-Benefit Analysis?

A business-case analysis or cost-benefit analysis can help agencies ensure they are using public funds most effectively and preparing to meet future performance goals.[16] The National Research Council, in a 2004 report on federal facilities investments, maintained that a business-case analysis of investments can make clear underlying assumptions, alternatives considered, the full range of costs and benefits, and the potential consequences for an organization and its missions.[17] Additionally, we have noted in prior work that a cost-benefit analysis can be a useful tool to inform decision making. It can provide an analytic framework that decision makers can use to consider factors in a systematic manner and clarify what is and is not known about effects.[18] OMB, similarly, has issued guidelines for agencies to consider when conducting a cost-benefit analysis of federal programs.[19] These guidelines are intended to promote efficient resource allocation through well-informed decision making, and in them OMB recommends that agencies conduct a sound cost-benefit analysis before initiating any long-term project that extends 3 or more years into the future. According to OMB's guidance, such analysis should include a policy rationale, explicit assumptions, an evaluation of the alternatives, and a plan to verify program results.

Consolidation initiatives based on a clearly presented business-case or cost-benefit analysis, grounded in accurate and reliable data, can provide a data-driven rationale for why an agency is undertaking a particular initiative and show stakeholders that a range of alternatives has been considered. However, agencies may find it difficult to obtain sufficiently accurate data necessary to calculate the full potential costs and benefits associated with a consolidation initiative. We have previously reported, for instance, that agencies across the federal government have faced

---

[16]A business-case analysis or cost-benefit analysis is a comparative analysis that presents facts and supporting details among competing alternatives. See GAO, *Cost Estimating and Assessment Guide: Best Practices for Developing and Managing Capital Program Costs*, GAO-09-3SP (Washington, D.C.: March 2009).

[17]National Research Council, *Investments in Federal Facilities: Asset Management Strategies for the 21st Century* (Washington, D.C., National Academies Press, 2004).

[18]GAO, *Highlights of an Expert Panel: The Benefits and Costs of Highway and Transit Investments*, GAO-05-423SP (Washington, D.C.: May 6, 2005).

[19]OMB, *Guidelines and Discount Rates for Benefit-Cost Analysis of Federal Programs*, OMB Circular A-94 (Washington, D.C.: Oct. 29, 1992).

challenges employing systematic cost-accounting practices in their operations.[20] A lack of these practices within agencies makes it more difficult for them to collect the data necessary to calculate precisely the costs and benefits of a consolidation. This limitation can increase a consolidation's risk and an agency's vulnerability to unintended consequences, such as increased costs or heightened stakeholder skepticism.

A lack of accurate data should not, however, necessarily preclude agencies from considering the costs and benefits of consolidation. Agencies can work to analyze the information they have at hand on likely costs and benefits, as an analysis of this information can reasonably indicate the likelihood that a consolidation will offer more benefits than costs. Agencies can also use sensitivity analysis to determine whether costs and benefits within certain error ranges will result in net benefits. Sensitivity analysis examines the effect of changing assumptions and ground rules on estimated costs and benefits and helps decision makers choose between alternatives. On the other hand, if agencies cannot definitely conclude that benefits will outweigh costs, or an analysis of the sensitivity to error of key data used to calculate costs and benefits suggests that a consolidation initiative faces considerable risks, they may need to consider alternatives other than consolidation.

- For example, we have previously reported that DOD established a structured process for obtaining and analyzing data during the BRAC 2005 round. DOD used its Cost of Base Realignment Actions (COBRA) model to provide consistency in potential cost, savings, and return-on-investment estimates for closure and realignment options.[21] COBRA provides for several key outputs that may influence the decision-making process, including (1) estimated costs for such factors as personnel severance, moving costs, or military construction over the implementation period; (2) estimated savings for personnel position eliminations, or reduced operations and maintenance costs over that same period; (3) the "payback" time required for estimated

---

[20]For example, see GAO, *Human Capital: DOD Needs Better Internal Controls and Visibility over Costs for Implementing Its National Security Personnel System,* GAO-07-851 (Washington, D.C.: July 16, 2007) and *Financial Management: NOAA Needs to Better Document Its Policies and Procedures for Providing Management and Administration Services,* GAO-11-226 (Washington, D.C.: Jan. 31, 2011).

[21]GAO-11-520T.

cumulative savings to outweigh cumulative costs for the actions; (4) net annual recurring savings; and (5) the net present value of BRAC actions, calculated over a 20-year time frame. We examined the model as part of our review of the 2005 and prior BRAC rounds and found it to be a generally reasonable estimator for comparing potential costs and savings among alternatives. The model provides important input into the selection process as decision makers weigh the financial implications of decisions regarding the suitability of various closure and realignment options. However, COBRA does not represent budget-quality estimates that are developed once BRAC decisions are made and detailed implementation plans are developed. On the basis of our assessment of the BRAC 2005 round, actual costs and savings were different from the BRAC Commission's initial estimates. As we testified in March 2012, BRAC onetime implementation costs rose to about $35.1 billion using DOD's fiscal year 2011 budget data compared with the Commission's initial estimate of $21 billion in fiscal year 2005. Also, we testified in 2012 that DOD expects to realize annual net recurring savings of $3.8 billion, a decrease of 9.5 percent compared to the Commission's estimate in 2005. We further testified that our analysis shows that the 20-year net present value is about $9.9 billion, a decrease of 73 percent, compared to the Commission's estimate of $36 billion in 2005.[22]

- VA and DOD officials told us that the departments' decision to consolidate their two health care facilities in North Chicago, Illinois, was based on a variety of factors, ranging from the facilities' proximity to each other to the opportunity created by the VA's having upgraded hospital infrastructure and identified clinical space with excess

---

[22]GAO, *Military Base Realignments and Closures: Key Factors Contributing to BRAC 2005 Results,* GAO-12-513T (Washington, D.C.: Mar. 8, 2012). As we have previously reported, we and the BRAC Commission believe that DOD's net annual recurring savings estimates are overstated because they include savings from eliminating military personnel positions without corresponding decreases in end-strength. DOD disagrees with our position. See also, GAO, *Military Base Realignments and Closures: Estimated Costs Have Increased While Savings Estimates Have Decreased Since Fiscal Year 2009,* GAO-10-98R (Washington, D.C.: Nov. 13, 2009).

capacity, and the Navy's need to replace its aging facility.[23] The two departments had earlier noted in a February 2009 analysis that the decision to consolidate the two facilities into the Captain James A. Lovell Federal Health Care Center (FHCC) in North Chicago was based on a sequential decision making process whereby each decision and cost-benefit analysis led to the next set of questions and options. In the analysis, they also laid out the consolidation's three sequential phases. In the first phase, the two departments developed a sharing relationship that included the consolidation of select medical services and the establishment of common administrative functions such as reimbursement methodology. In the second phase, they forged a network relationship that included VA's construction of new facilities, the consolidation of more medical services, and the development of additional reimbursement methodology. VA and DOD officials determined that the reduction of operating costs and full-time equivalents in the first two phases saved a total of $11.2 million, while allowing the two hospitals to maintain a high quality of care based on established metrics. VA and DOD also estimated that phase three, which includes the Navy's construction of new facilities and the opening of the fully-integrated FHCC, will lead to onetime construction avoidance savings of $67 million and annual recurring savings of $19.7 million.

- Census officials told us that as the bureau was weighing alternatives for consolidating its field office structure, it developed costs and benefits for each alternative. Census officials told us that they had some difficulty identifying the consolidation's costs, but ultimately compiled a list of costs for the selected alternative. Costs ranged from relocation expenses for employees who would remain with the agency, to separation incentives and severance pay for those who could not or would not remain with the agency, to training costs for

---

[23]DOD and VA integrated the Naval Health Clinic Great Lakes and the North Chicago VA Medical Center and are operating a system of healthcare known as the DOD/VA Medical Facility Demonstration Project, Federal Health Care Center (FHCC) from 2010 to 2015 pursuant to statutory authority. 10 U.S.C. § 1104; 38 U.S.C. § 8111; Duncan Hunter National Defense Authorization Act for Fiscal Year 2009, Pub. L. No. 110-417, § 706, 122 Stat. 4356, 4500 (2008); National Defense Authorization Act for Fiscal Year 2010, Pub. L. No. 111-84, §§ 1701-1706, 123 Stat 2190, 2567–2574 (2009). These provisions authorize the FHCC to provide health care services to VA and DOD beneficiaries, consistent with applicable policies of both departments. To accomplish the missions of both departments in this VA/DOD integration, the FHCC will support both VA/DOD Healthcare and DOD Operational readiness missions.

new positions. These costs totaled approximately $30 million over 3 fiscal years. Census also identified $15 million to $18 million in potentially recurring savings, which it attributed to the closure of six offices and the net reduction of 186 full-time equivalent positions across the field structure. A Census official said that such data helped to persuade stakeholders of the consolidation's value.

- Sufficiently reliable data, however, are hindering OMB's efforts to create an inventory of data centers and estimate cost savings as agencies consolidate their data centers and move from housing data on site to cloud-computing solutions.[24] Such a move to cloud computing can allow agencies to obtain computing services while freeing themselves from the burdens and costs of maintaining computing infrastructure. To help agencies improve their use of data centers, OMB is leading an effort to create a shared-services marketplace as part of a data center consolidation initiative. According to OMB, this initiative could lead to $3 billion in savings by 2015 as well as improve the efficiency, performance, and environmental footprint of federal data center activities.[25] To help agencies plan for their data center consolidations, OMB directed them to first complete a data center inventory and a consolidation plan. Specifically, the inventories were to include descriptions of the assets present within individual data centers, as well as information about the physical data center. The consolidation plans were to address key elements, including goals, approaches, schedules, cost-benefit calculations, and risk management plans. However, we found that the majority of the agencies did not complete their inventories or consolidation plans, due in part to a lack of available data. For example, 19 of the 24 agencies we reviewed reported that it was challenging to obtain power-usage data. Certain agency facilities do not have power-metering capabilities, making estimations of power use necessary. We concluded that moving forward to consolidate obviously redundant or underused centers is nonetheless warranted and should result in

---

[24]Cloud computing is location-independent computing, whereby shared servers provide resources, software, and data to computers and other devices on demand, as with the electricity grid. In May 2010, GAO issued a report on federal cloud computing efforts. See *Information Security: Federal Guidance Needed to Address Control Issues with Implementing Cloud Computing*, GAO-10-513 (Washington, D.C.: May 27, 2010).

[25]In GAO-11-565, we reported that 14 agencies initially reported savings between 2011 and 2015 from the data center consolidation initiative of $700 million, but actual savings may be even higher because 12 of those agencies' estimates were incomplete.

immediate cost savings and increased efficiency. However, these data gaps place agencies at an increased risk of being ill prepared to manage such a significant transformation. We raised concerns that OMB cannot be assured that agencies are providing a sound baseline for estimating consolidation savings or accurately measuring their progress until those inventories and plans are complete and there is a better understanding of the validity of the agencies' data, and we recommended that OMB require agencies to complete the missing elements in their respective consolidation plans.[26] OMB generally agreed with our report but did not comment on the recommendation. In July 2011, OMB directed agencies to complete all missing elements in their respective consolidation plans by the end of fiscal year 2011. In March 2012, OMB further established an annual requirement for agencies to complete missing elements from their plans and to submit an updated plan by the end of every fiscal year.

- A past independent evaluation by the MITRE Corporation recommended that EPA consolidate its laboratories as a means to improve the efficiency and effectiveness of its operations, and in 2006, EPA's Chief Financial Officer requested that EPA develop a plan for reducing laboratory costs through their consolidation.[27] In prior work, we reported that EPA lacks sufficiently complete and reliable data on which to base decisions about the management of its laboratories. For example, we reported that EPA does not use public and commercial benchmarks to calculate usage rates for its laboratories. Instead, EPA measures laboratory usage on the basis of subjective interviews with local laboratory officials.[28] We recommended that EPA improve the completeness and reliability of operating-cost and other data needed to manage its real property, and if it determined that another independent study of its laboratories' management and operation was needed, include alternative options

---

[26]GAO-11-565.

[27]EPA tasked the MITRE Corporation to perform an independent evaluation of its laboratories to be used by the agency as one of the inputs in developing a report to Congress. The MITRE Corporation is a not-for-profit organization chartered to work in the public interest with expertise in systems engineering, information technology, operational concepts, and enterprise modernization.

[28]GAO, *Environmental Protection Agency: To Better Fulfill Its Mission, EPA Needs a More Coordinated Approach to Managing Its Laboratories*, GAO-11-347 (Washington, D.C.: July 25, 2011).

for organizing its laboratories' infrastructure, including consolidation. EPA said that it will work internally to upgrade and validate internal operating costs and other metrics, and that it is preparing a work assignment for the National Academy of Sciences to study EPA's laboratories. EPA stated that the study will consider alternate approaches for organizing the laboratories' infrastructure.

- We have reported that as more agencies join ICASS, State has realized savings through economies of scale. However, we have also reported that ICASS and its customer agencies generally have insufficient data to perform a meaningful cost analysis to quantify the potential cost savings to individual agencies or the government as a whole from consolidating services. Responses to a survey we conducted for our 2012 report showed that agencies that have opted out of ICASS services have frequently cited lower costs as a reason for their decision, but many indicated that they had no basis to judge the relative costs of ICASS and non-ICASS services or did not respond to a question on this issue. Furthermore, State's ICASS cost data and other agencies' non-ICASS cost data are generally not comparable, which renders the cost implications for an agency's joining ICASS unclear. Without data that can help it quantify potential cost savings, ICASS management is poorly positioned to demonstrate to other agencies that greater participation in ICASS services is in their own interest or that of the U.S. government overall.[29] We suggested that Congress may wish to consider requiring agencies to participate in ICASS services unless they provide a business case to show that they can obtain these services outside of ICASS without increasing overall costs to the U.S. government or they show that their mission cannot be achieved within ICASS. We also recommended that, where agencies are able to demonstrate, through a compelling business case, that they can provide a service more efficiently than the existing State ICASS provider without adverse effects on the overall government budget, the Secretary of State and the Administrator of the U.S. Agency for International Development (USAID) allow the creation of new ICASS service providers, in lieu of State, to provide administrative services to the other agencies at individual posts. State and USAID generally concurred with these recommendations.

---

[29]GAO-12-317.

How Can the Up-Front Costs Associated with the Consolidation Be Funded?

Physical infrastructure and management function consolidation initiatives often have up-front costs, and agencies must pay them before they can realize any intended gains or savings. For example, agencies may need to pay for equipment and furniture moves or fund employee transfers and buyouts, and agencies often find it challenging to obtain the funds necessary to pay for these up-front costs. A lack of up-front funding can prevent a potentially beneficial initiative from getting off the ground or derail an initiative already underway. In fact, our prior work on real property management has shown that a lack of funding for up-front costs is one of the most important reasons why many initiatives are never implemented.[30]

- In previous work on the BRAC process, we noted that the costs associated with closing bases can be significant. Congress has provided DOD with a dedicated mechanism to help meet the challenges of paying for BRAC's significant up-front costs: the Department of Defense Base Closure Account was established to fund base closures in the 1988 round; the Department of Defense Closure Account 1990 was established to fund base closures in the 1991, 1993, and 1995 rounds; and the Department of Defense Base Closure Account 2005 was established to fund base closures in the 2005 round. Congress, recognizing the complexities of realigning and closing bases, allowed DOD the flexibility to allocate funds by military service, budget function, and installation. Additionally, other revenues, including revenues generated from land sales, were required to be deposited into these accounts to offset closure and realignment costs.

- As previously mentioned, Census collected data on costs and benefits as it weighed alternatives for consolidating its field office structure. The bureau's Chief Financial Officer noted that the bureau is finding it challenging to pay for the up-front costs, as it plans to absorb them and not pass them on to customers by charging higher fees for survey administration. He said that Census is planning to pay for the consolidation's up-front costs with money from Census's working

---

[30]See, for example, GAO, *Federal Real Property: Overreliance on Leasing Contributed to High-Risk Designation,* GAO-11-879T (Washington, D.C.: Aug. 4, 2011).

capital fund.[31] Census said that, as there will be no additional charges to customers, Census will use balances from its working capital fund collections while simultaneously conserving resources and finding efficiencies within the fund to pay for the consolidation's up-front costs. Another Census official noted that Census expects to realize cost savings from liquidating regional office space and reducing the number of employees in the consolidated regional office structure. However, Census will not fully realize these savings until fiscal year 2014.

- We have reported that 11 of the agencies involved in the data center consolidation initiative have found it challenging to fund their consolidation efforts.[32] For example, one agency noted that having to fund efforts long before any savings would be realized was difficult. There is no standard method by which agencies are paying for these up-front data center consolidation costs. Some agencies are using working capital funds while others use funds appropriated through the annual budget process; other agencies are using a combination of the two. The Department of Commerce, in its 2011 data center consolidation plan, noted that it has worked to overcome up-front cost challenges and more effectively obtain funds to meet its data center consolidation requirements by streamlining information technology operations and by having its data center consolidation project team demonstrate the cost benefit of the initiative to the department's executive management.

A former OMB official said that centrally administered incentive funds could be effective in helping agencies initiate a consolidation, particularly cross-government consolidations, such as those that were pursued under

---

[31]A working capital fund is a type of intragovernmental revolving fund that generally finances the centralized provision of common services within an agency, such as building security or human capital management. Receipts come primarily from other government agencies, programs, or activities. See GAO, *Principles of Federal Appropriations Law,* GAO-08-978SP (Washington, D.C.: September 2008). Census's working capital fund contains money that the bureau collects for providing management and administrative services to its internal divisions and survey support services for other federal and nonfederal entities. See GAO, *Intragovernmental Revolving Funds: Commerce Departmental and Census Working Capital Funds Should Better Reflect Key Operating Principles,* GAO-12-56 (Washington, D.C.: Nov. 18, 2011).

[32]GAO-11-565.

the Lines of Business initiative.[33] As we have previously reported, the administration is undertaking one such effort by having OMB manage the Partnership Fund for Program Integrity Innovation, a fund that provides federal agencies money to pilot projects and evaluations that test ideas for improving the delivery of federal assistance programs administered through state and local governments.[34] The fund is intended to help agencies, among other goals, improve administrative efficiency and is expected to help agencies achieve total cost savings that are equal to or greater than the fund's $32.5 million appropriation. Additionally, we have reported that the Department of Housing and Urban Development (HUD) has developed a centrally administered fund to support its Transformation Initiative, a multifaceted and multiyear effort intended to reexamine how HUD does business by focusing on improving performance, replacing outdated information technology systems, evaluating programs, and streamlining processes.[35] In fiscal year 2010, HUD received authorization from Congress to transfer up to 1 percent of the budgets from selected program offices to a Transformation Initiative fund that is intended to support projects that improve the overall performance of the agency, including a few project areas that are specifically expected to improve efficiency.[36] Furthermore, in September 2011, we recommended that the Director of OMB work with Congress and federal agencies to develop proposals for funding mechanisms that assist federal agencies with the up-front costs associated with longer-term efficiency improvement projects.[37] We requested an update on the status of this recommendation in April 2012. However, OMB has not yet indicated how it will address the recommendation.

---

[33]The Bush administration's Lines of Business initiative was designed to improve the federal government's use of information technology and better business practices. In the spring of 2004, OMB announced the formation of Lines of Business task forces. The task forces analyzed data to identify ways where services could integrate common information technology and electronic government-related practices across agencies into a single unified standard. OMB planned to form "centers of excellence" or "shared service vendors" for each line of business to manage common functions and tasks across agencies.

[34]GAO, *Streamlining Government: Key Practices from Select Efficiency Initiatives Should Be Shared Governmentwide*, GAO-11-908 (Washington, D.C.: Sept. 30, 2011).

[35]GAO-11-908.

[36]Consolidated Appropriations Act, 2010, Pub. L. No. 111-117, 123 Stat. 3034, 3093 (2010).

[37]GAO-11-908.

GAO-12-542 Consolidation Proposals

The need for agencies to consolidate incompatible information technology systems can be one of the most challenging aspects of a consolidation, particularly if the initiative crosses departmental lines. We have previously reported that individual agencies have hundreds of incompatible networks and systems and that the maintenance of these legacy systems is costly. We have found that even now the architectures agencies are developing are duplicative, poorly integrated, unnecessarily costly to maintain and interface, and unable to respond quickly to shifting environmental factors.[38]

- In the early 2000s, when the payroll systems consolidation initiative was announced, many of the agencies' payroll systems were nearing the end of their estimated life cycles. OMB capitalized on the situation by not authorizing agencies, other than the four chosen payroll service providers, to spend money on modernizing their payroll systems, thereby leveraging the shift to the selected payroll providers. However, OPM officials also said that funding for systems modernization for the four remaining payroll service providers, which was promised at the outset of the payroll consolidation initiative, has not materialized. They noted that this lack of funding for systems modernization is a major problem and puts the long-term viability of the consolidated federal payroll services system at risk.

Who Are the Consolidation Stakeholders, and How Will They Be Affected?

Consolidation success depends on a wide range of factors, including getting incentives right for those affected by the consolidation. Stakeholders often view a consolidation as working against their own interests. For example, agency clients and customers may have concerns about potential reduction in service or access to agency officials. Contractors providing services or systems to multiple agencies may be concerned that consolidation will result in fewer agency customers and create a situation where they are competing with agencies to provide management or administrative services. Congress, which authorizes and funds federal agency operations, may be sensitive to these concerns, especially when Congressional members' constituencies are adversely affected. Moreover, stakeholders frequently raise valid concerns on the basis of their familiarity with an agency's operations, and the concerns need to be addressed openly and objectively. Failure to effectively engage with stakeholders and understand and address their views can

---

[38]GAO-11-318SP.

undermine or derail the initiative. To that end, it is critical that agencies identify who the relevant stakeholders are and develop a two-way communication strategy that both addresses their concerns and conveys the rationale for and overarching benefits associated with a consolidation initiative. We have previously reported that communication is not just "pushing the message out," but should facilitate a two-way, honest exchange with and allow for feedback from employees, customers, and other stakeholders.[39] Full agreement among stakeholders is relatively uncommon because stakeholders' interests can differ significantly; a comprehensive two-way communication strategy is central to forming the effective external and internal partnerships that are vital to the success of any organization.

External Stakeholders

Closing regional offices or facilities, which may be necessary to generate cost savings or efficiency gains, may engender strong opposition from local residents and the population served by the office. We have previously described how independent commissions, which by design are to be less subject to parochial or political pressures, can more easily effect change, ensure that data collection and analysis are efficient and objective, and implement recommendations quickly.[40]

- For example, DOD and BRAC Commission officials cite the establishment of an independent commission and nomination of commissioners by the President, in consultation with congressional leadership, as one of the key elements that contributed to DOD's ability to eliminate excess capacity by closing or realigning military bases. In addition, the President and Congress have to accept or reject the commission's report in its entirety. More recently, we reported that an independent commission or governmentwide task

---

[39]GAO, *Results-Oriented Cultures: Implementation Steps to Assist Mergers and Organizational Transformations*, GAO-03-669 (Washington, D.C. July 2, 2003).

[40]GAO/NSIAD/RCED-98-23. Also, in February 2012, the House passed as amended H.R. 1734, the Civilian Property Realignment Act. The legislation would establish an independent Civilian Property Realignment Commission to identify opportunities for the federal government to reduce its inventory of civilian real property and reduce costs. The legislation would require each federal agency to submit current data to the General Services Administration and OMB regarding the agency's federal civilian real property and to recommend sales or other dispositions of federal property, reductions in civilian property inventory, and operational efficiencies.

force might be necessary to help overcome stakeholder influences in deciding how to dispose of unneeded real property.[41]

An effective and ongoing communication strategy tailored to address different stakeholder groups and their concerns is also essential.

- For example, IRS and Census officials pursued a data-driven communication strategy that started well in advance of their regional office closures. Census officials said they used data to demonstrate to local elected officials how streamlining operations would allow Census to save money and conduct surveys more efficiently. In addition, Census developed scripts and timelines to roll out the announcement so key officials could deliver the same information and message throughout the country at the same time (see fig. 1). Census officials said their communication strategy allowed them to present a unified front and consistent information.

---

[41]GAO-11-520T.

GAO-12-542 Consolidation Proposals

Figure 1: Timeline for Census Bureau Consolidation Plan Announcement

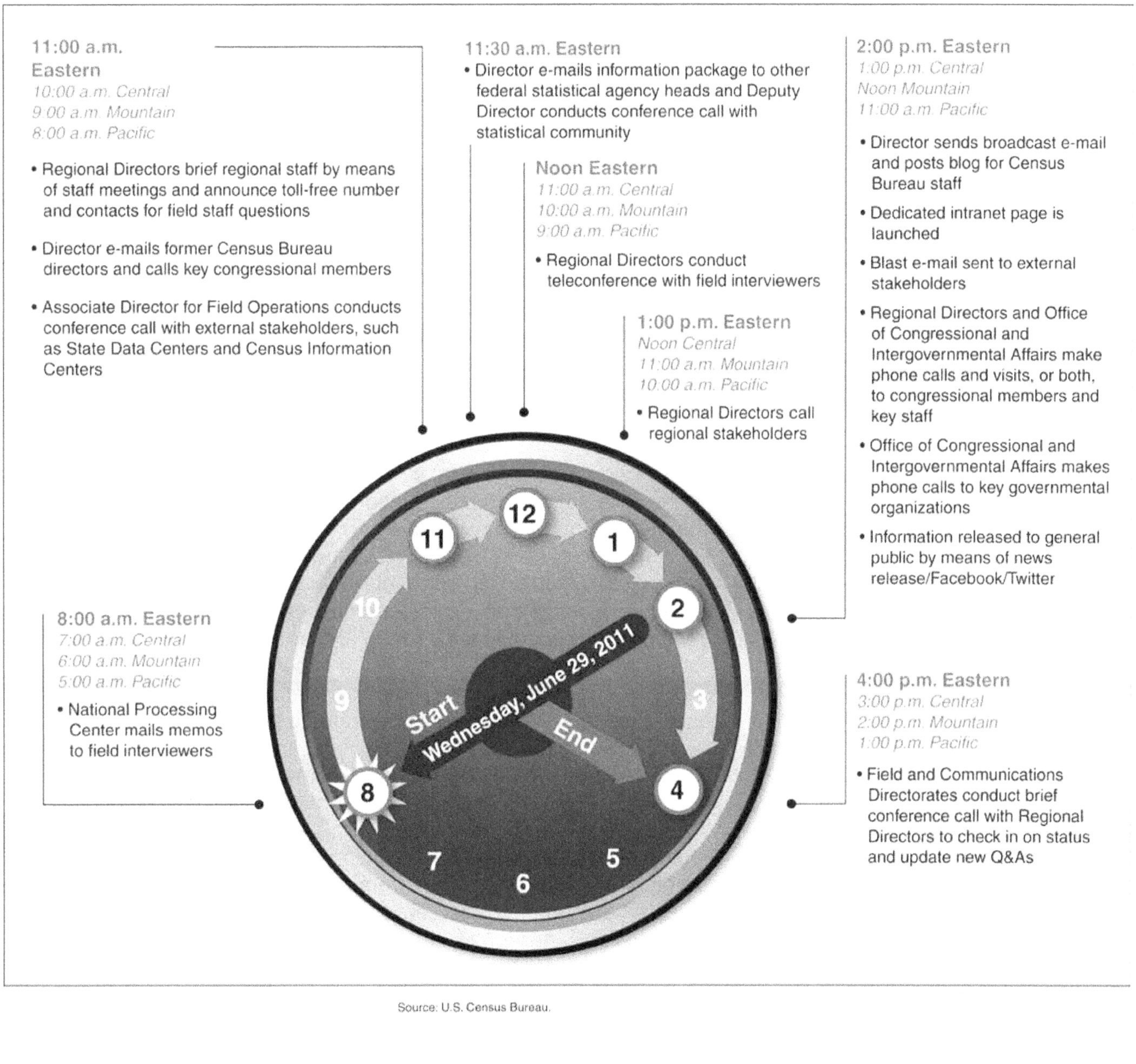

11:00 a.m. Eastern
10:00 a.m. Central
9:00 a.m. Mountain
8:00 a.m. Pacific

- Regional Directors brief regional staff by means of staff meetings and announce toll-free number and contacts for field staff questions
- Director e-mails former Census Bureau directors and calls key congressional members
- Associate Director for Field Operations conducts conference call with external stakeholders, such as State Data Centers and Census Information Centers

11:30 a.m. Eastern
- Director e-mails information package to other federal statistical agency heads and Deputy Director conducts conference call with statistical community

Noon Eastern
11:00 a.m. Central
10:00 a.m. Mountain
9:00 a.m. Pacific

- Regional Directors conduct teleconference with field interviewers

1:00 p.m. Eastern
Noon Central
11:00 a.m. Mountain
10:00 a.m. Pacific

- Regional Directors call regional stakeholders

2:00 p.m. Eastern
1:00 p.m. Central
Noon Mountain
11:00 a.m. Pacific

- Director sends broadcast e-mail and posts blog for Census Bureau staff
- Dedicated intranet page is launched
- Blast e-mail sent to external stakeholders
- Regional Directors and Office of Congressional and Intergovernmental Affairs make phone calls and visits, or both, to congressional members and key staff
- Office of Congressional and Intergovernmental Affairs makes phone calls to key governmental organizations
- Information released to general public by means of news release/Facebook/Twitter

8:00 a.m. Eastern
7:00 a.m. Central
6:00 a.m. Mountain
5:00 a.m. Pacific

- National Processing Center mails memos to field interviewers

4:00 p.m. Eastern
3:00 p.m. Central
2:00 p.m. Mountain
1:00 p.m. Pacific

- Field and Communications Directorates conduct brief conference call with Regional Directors to check in on status and update new Q&As

Start Wednesday, June 29, 2011 End

Source: U.S. Census Bureau.

- To address congressional concerns about processing centers closing in their districts, IRS officials reported they developed a communication strategy based on data showing that they could close one site every other year without adversely affecting operations, due in large part to the steady increase in electronic filing and concurrent decline in paper filing of tax returns. Also, once the decision had been made to close processing centers, IRS took steps to communicate with taxpayers about changes in filing locations through a variety of media including websites, informational packages sent to taxpayers, and tax practitioner forums.

Internal Stakeholders

Agency officials reported that a comprehensive communication strategy that involves employees is a key component of any consolidation effort. Consolidations of physical infrastructure or management support functions often generate uncertainty for agency employees through job loss, relocation, or considerable changes in the way jobs are done. Regular and early communication facilitates a two-way exchange, which allows for feedback and tailored information to meet employees' specific needs. The communication can help to build trust and an understanding of the planned change, potentially defusing the opposition while strengthening commitment to the effort.

- Once IRS determined it was closing processing sites, agency officials and representatives from the National Treasury Employees Union said they negotiated how shutting down individual sites would occur and what mitigation measures would be available to employees. A variety of communication channels including websites, town hall meetings, and newsletters helped employees keep abreast of dates and the consolidation's progress. IRS also posted information on its internal websites regarding the range of services available to employees losing their jobs, such as separation packages, reassignment opportunities, retraining and placement assistance, and counseling. In addition, IRS began hiring limited term or temporary employees at sites slated for closure, allowing the agency to communicate realistic expectations about job duration.

- Census officials also reported developing a comprehensive employee communication strategy. The strategy's intent was to address morale issues among employees keeping their jobs but with new or different responsibilities, as well as employees relocating or losing their jobs. The week following the consolidation's announcement, the Census Bureau Director visited the six closing regional offices to answer employees' questions and listen to concerns. Human resource representatives followed up quickly with regional office employees to discuss these concerns. Three months later, the representatives held video conferences with individual employees to explain the early retirement and buyout process. Census also created a consolidation intranet site accessible to all Census employees that contains a variety of information, including internal job postings. In addition, Census electronically distributes a monthly consolidation newsletter and has established an "800" telephone number employees can call with consolidation questions. Census has dedicated itself to answering all questions submitted through the 800 number and posting all questions and answers to the intranet site.

Concerns about ceding control in a new consolidated environment of shared services can also be a major challenge. A report we issued in 1980 looking at barriers to closing regional offices cited management resistance on the basis of concerns that participating in shared service arrangements would diminish their control and lead to a decrease in service.[42] For example, we reported that many agencies were reluctant to adopt automatic airline ticket payment plans and teleticketing procedures even though these techniques had been shown to be cost effective and subsequently have become the norm. Agencies had developed their own travel systems to support important aspects of their operations, and many managers did not believe that a common support arrangement would satisfy their unique needs. Thirty years later, the same general issue resonates.

- A former OPM official involved with the payroll consolidation initiative said that even though the payroll effort was an intellectually simple concept, it still required "brute force" to execute. She said that agencies resisted the effort because they claimed they had a type of payment necessitating a unique payroll system. To address these concerns and devise solutions, OPM established a Payroll Advisory Council that included representatives from the provider agencies and client agencies. The council met quarterly to develop migration and business processes. OPM officials said the council was a valuable vehicle for bringing together key stakeholders and encouraging them to feel they were part of the process. They said it helped get people on the same page and motivated them to move the project forward.

Employee resistance to cultural change is a particularly thorny issue when consolidation involves more than one agency. Constructing a new organizational culture that respects the core values of the involved organizations and is welcoming to all employees is critical to the success

---

[42]GAO, *Streamlining the Federal Field Structure: Potential Opportunities, Barriers, and Actions That Can Be Taken*, FPCD-80-4 (Washington, D.C.: Aug. 5, 1980).

of a multiagency consolidation effort. Our prior work has shown that many transformations fail because the cultures of the components were not fully understood or considered.[43] Thus, managers need to understand the different cultures that are coming together, and the steps that can be taken to establish a common culture.[44]

- Federal Health Care Center (FHCC) officials reported that the center has sought to address the challenges of cultural integration through a wide variety of actions and approaches, such as involving all staff in establishing the mission, vision, and goal statements; creating its first strategic plan; and blending previously unique organizational celebrations and recognition events. According to the officials, ongoing assessments of progress with cultural integration have been maintained through staff satisfaction and climate surveys, as well as frequent communication opportunities with leadership through all-hands town hall meetings and other communication venues. From fiscal years 2011 through 2012, FHCC improved in 12 of 13 measured categories including work group effectiveness and leadership cohesion; however, its score dropped slightly in the work group cohesion category. In addition, VA and DOD, through FHCC staff, use a staff satisfaction benchmark as one measure to assess the center's integration, a benchmark that has been met. Officials noted that establishing a common culture from two distinct and firmly established entities like the VA and the United States Navy has been challenging. However, with a focus from leadership and the actions mentioned above, officials said the center has seen progress in establishing its own common culture.

To What Extent Do Plans Show That Change Management Practices Will Be Used to Implement the Consolidation?

Implementing large-scale organizational mergers, acquisitions, and transformation initiatives, such as consolidations, are not simple endeavors and require the concentrated efforts of both leadership and employees to accomplish new organizational goals. As we have previously reported, productivity and effectiveness may actually decline in the period immediately following a private sector merger and acquisition.[45] This happens for a number of reasons including that

---

[43]GAO-03-669.

[44]Peter Frumkin, *Making Public Sector Mergers Work: Lessons Learned* (Arlington, Va.: IBM Center for The Business of Government, August 2003).

[45]GAO-03-293SP.

attention is concentrated on critical and immediate integration issues and diverted from longer-term mission issues. In addition, employees and managers inevitably worry about their place in the changed organization.

As part of our body of work on organizational mergers, acquisitions, and other transformations, we recommended that to minimize the duration and the significance of any reduced productivity and effectiveness, agencies should have an implementation plan that includes essential change management practices such as active, engaged leadership of executives at the highest possible levels; a dedicated implementation team that can be held accountable for change; and a strategy for capturing best practices, measuring progress toward the established goals of the consolidation, retaining key talent, and assessing and mitigating risk, among others.[46] Appendix III has a list of key change management practices.

Will Top Leadership Be Engaged in Driving the Consolidation?

Whether consolidations originate from within an agency in response to changing conditions or outside pressures, or from the most senior levels of government, it is essential that top government and agency leaders are committed to the consolidation and play a lead role in executing it. As we have previously reported, leadership must set the direction, pace, and tone and provide a clear, consistent rationale to agency staff to increase the likelihood of a successful consolidation.[47]

- According to OPM officials who managed the implementation of the payroll consolidation initiative, the initiative required sustained White House and OMB involvement as well as the creation of the advisory council discussed above that brought together the key players from each of the agencies.

- The plan to consolidate Census Bureau regional offices originated among senior-level Census officials. Specifically, the director, deputy director, and Field Division's senior management developed various options on the basis of different configurations and multiple plans. According to Census officials, they maintained absolute secrecy during this planning stage, which they said allowed them to consider a range of options that may otherwise have encountered immediate

---

[46]GAO-03-293SP.

[47]GAO-03-239SP.

resistance. Once the Director of the Census Bureau decided on the new structure, the agency developed a communication strategy and informed key stakeholders, including relevant congressional members and staff, state and local elected officials, affected regional office staff, and then all other regional Census Bureau employees. Census leaders noted that they are now involved with every implementation step of their internally-driven effort.

- We recently observed that in light of current efforts to reduce the federal budget deficit, which include significant proposed cuts in the budgets of most departments and agencies, including EPA, the agency will need to more effectively use its scientific and laboratory resources across the agency to ensure the agency is best positioned to fulfill the critical scientific work for its core mission.[48] Although independent evaluations have identified problems with EPA's laboratories' operations and management and called for improved planning, coordination, and leadership, as well as consolidation of laboratories, EPA has not appointed a top science official with responsibility and authority over all of the agency's research, science, and technical activities. Instead, these activities remain fragmented and largely uncoordinated, reflecting the independent organizational and management structures of the 15 senior officials charged with managing the scientific work performed at each laboratory. To improve cohesion in the management and operation of EPA's laboratories, we recommended that EPA establish a top-level science official with the authority and responsibility to coordinate, oversee, and make management decisions regarding major scientific activities throughout the agency, including the work of all program and regional laboratories. In response to our recommendation, EPA proposed to increase the responsibilities of its science advisor. However, it is not clear that this will fully address the issue and it may ultimately introduce additional challenges for EPA.

Will a Dedicated Implementation Team Lead the Consolidation?

We have previously reported that successful major merger and transformation efforts dedicate a strong and stable consolidation implementation team to lead the day-to-day management of a transformation initiative.

- For example, IRS determined that the oversight, planning, and implementation of its consolidation should be centralized. The agency

---

[48]GAO-11-347.

assigned responsibility for the implementation of its processing site consolidation plan to two offices within the Wage & Investment Division—the Customer Account Services Project Management Office and the Submission Processing Project Management Office. IRS officials said that it was important to have the same people involved throughout the process, and they noted that it was also helpful to establish time lines. They also used action plans to detail needed tasks and issues encountered during the consolidation process. The plans contained specific action items, dates, and responsible parties to help ensure accountability. IRS executives and managers reported that they met frequently during the consolidation process to discuss the action plans and progress made. The IRS also developed website resources to help the implementation team communicate changes to the rest of the agency.

A 2007 audit conducted by the Treasury Inspector General for Tax Administration (TIGTA) found that the IRS implementation team helped to ensure a smooth transition during the consolidation.[49] Specifically, TIGTA noted that the implementation team developed detailed plans that contained specific action items, dates, and responsible parties to help ensure accountability. The implementation team also met frequently with IRS executives and managers to discuss issues and progress made and communicated often with employees. TIGTA also found that the reduction in the number of processing sites did not adversely affect the processing of individual tax returns, and the IRS continued to have successful filing seasons during the consolidation process. They reported that IRS efforts to maintain high productivity and minimize the effect on taxpayers during the transition were generally successful.

- OPM officials credited the sustained involvement of top leadership at the White House and OMB and a small, but dedicated, implementation team as driving factors in the payroll consolidation initiative. To oversee the payroll initiative, OPM created a Program Management Office, which consisted of the payroll initiative director, five full-time staff, and three contractors. The project director reported directly to the director of OPM. One OPM official emphasized that these were dedicated staff that spent all of their time on the project, rather than as an additional duty.

---

[49]Treasury Inspector General for Tax Administration, *Consolidation of Tax Return Processing Sites is Progressing Effectively, but Improved Project Management is Needed,* 2007-40-165 (Washington, D.C.: Aug. 31, 2007).

Will the Implementation Plan Include Metrics to Measure Progress toward the Consolidation's Goals?

We have previously reported that federal agencies engaging in large projects need to plan to monitor and evaluate their efforts to identify areas for improvement.[50] Reporting on these activities can help key decision makers within the agencies, as well as stakeholders, obtain feedback for improving both policy and operational effectiveness. Establishing implementation goals and milestone dates, and tracking progress toward those goals helps agency officials pinpoint performance shortfalls and suggest midcourse corrections, including any needed adjustments to the organization's future goals and milestones. Moreover, transparent reporting tools can help agencies manage stakeholder expectations about how much is being spent, when savings will start to accrue, and whether the agency is meeting performance goals during the transition. Imprecise information can produce an unrealistic expectation of cost savings and undermine the public's trust.

Agencies consolidating physical infrastructure or management functions should plan to have metrics of success. These measures should show an organization's progress toward achieving an intended level of performance or results. Meaningful performance measures should also be limited to the vital few and cover multiple government priorities such as quality, timeliness, cost of service, customer service, and outcomes. Performance measurement systems need to include incentives for managers to strike the difficult balance among competing interests. One or two priorities, such as timeliness and cost, should not be overemphasized at the expense of others such as quality. Finally, measures need to provide managers and other stakeholders with timely, action-oriented information in a format that helps them make decisions that improve program performance.[51]

- For example, we reported that the performance plan VA and DOD developed to assess the provision of care and operations at the FHCC lacked transparency and may not provide a meaningful and accurate measure of success.[52] DOD and VA developed 15 integration benchmarks and their corresponding performance measures to help them monitor their performance in three main areas:

---

[50]GAO-03-669.

[51]GAO, *Tax Administration: IRS Needs to Further Refine Its Tax Filing Season Performance Measures,* GAO-03-143 (Washington, D.C.: Nov. 22, 2002).

[52]GAO-11-570.

patient and staff satisfaction; clinical and administrative functions; and external evaluation. FHCC staff developed a scorecard that calculates a single monthly summary score for the performance measures, which they planned to present at their regular Advisory Board meetings. We reported that although the scorecard has the potential to be useful in tracking performance results over time, it does not account for data collection variation; there are no designated target scores to indicate successful performance; and the scorecard initially contained a calculation error, all of which raised concerns about its ability to provide transparent, meaningful, and accurate information. To address these concerns, we recommended that the Secretaries of Veterans Affairs and Defense direct FHCC leadership to conduct further evaluation of the scorecard reporting tool and its methodology and make revisions that will better ensure the transparency and accuracy of the information reported. In response to our recommendations, the VA stated that it changed the calculation process for the scorecard's monthly score. Specifically, FHCC staff will populate the scorecard with a score for each measure every month using either data acquired that month, or the most recent available data for those measures.

- Census officials reported that they developed several financial and non-financial measures to assess their performance as they reorganize their regional structure. Officials also reported that they asked their survey clients to identify key concerns and risks, and then developed performance metrics to track those concerns. The measures they developed and plan to monitor include product quality, stakeholder satisfaction, productivity, transition costs, accrued savings, employee morale, and progress made toward meeting project milestones.

- According to TIGTA, IRS did not adequately monitor the costs and benefits that accrued as the consolidation plan was implemented and reported imprecise savings data.[53] The IRS could not provide reliable financial information on technology or personnel costs. The IRS also included savings resulting from electronic filing—and the subsequent decreased paper workload—in the savings it attributed to consolidation. To address TIGTA's concern, the agency developed a methodology for tracking costs and benefits related to site closures,

---

[53]Treasury Inspector General for Tax Administration, 2007-40-165.

which separated consolidation efforts from the effects of reduced paper workload due to electronic filing. Being able to accurately monitor costs and estimate when savings will begin to accrue is essential for providing sound information to congressional decision makers, maintaining public confidence in the agency's ability to carry out large operations, and ensuring that long-term, multimillion dollar projects proceed in the most efficient manner.

To monitor the success of those consolidation initiatives that involve one agency taking over a management function for another agency, agencies may find it helpful to measure customer service. Customer service measures can include customer access to services, wait times, accuracy, and other factors.[54]

- As the managing partner of the Human Resources Line of Business, OPM regularly assesses the four payroll providers on their ability to deliver on different business practices that customer agencies consider important, including customer relationship management. Practices are defined as proven management ideas that include techniques, methods, processes, or activities that can help an agency deliver outcomes. For example, the customer relationship management category includes the following practices: (1) understand and proactively address provider's customer needs; (2) proactively communicate and build relationships with provider's customers; (3) effectively respond to customer inquiries and requests; and (4) employ formal change management techniques to help customers identify and manage change. For each of the practices, OPM developed a set of yes-no assessment questions—such as, Does your provider make findings from customer surveys, interviews, focus groups, etc. available to you?—to substantiate a provider's ability to demonstrate the practice. Through this assessment, OPM can monitor and report on which customer relationship practices agency providers effectively employ and which need to be strengthened.

- State developed uniform service standards to measure service delivery at overseas posts; however, we found that these standards did not always address common concerns of overseas customers. For example, some agencies have raised concerns that ICASS service providers cannot meet their unique requirements, priority is given to

---

[54]GAO, *Managing for Results: Opportunities to Strengthen Customer Service Efforts,* GAO-11-44 (Washington, D.C.: Oct. 27, 2010).

some agencies over others, and their annual ICASS invoices contain billing errors, which require a significant amount of time to correct. State's performance reporting does not disaggregate results by customer agency, and as such, does not reflect the extent to which service delivery is inequitable across agencies, nor do State's metrics gauge progress on reducing the incidence of billing errors. To help ensure that State can more adroitly identify and address customer complaints, we recommended that it develop additional performance measures that gauge ICASS service providers' progress in resolving major sources of customer dissatisfaction.[55] State officials said they plan to increase the number of services for which performance data—including customer satisfaction data—are collected as part of an effort to better identify and meet the needs of customer agencies.

Will the Implementation Plan Include a Strategy for Attracting and Retaining Key Talent?

We have previously recommended that officials need a strategy to ensure that employees will have the appropriate skills to perform what may be new roles following consolidation. As described earlier, agencies may choose to consolidate infrastructure or functions because the old way of operating has become obsolete.

- For example, IRS consolidated processing sites to address the increase in electronic tax filing and subsequent decrease in paper filing. Officials from the National Treasury Employees Union said they worked with employees who were going to lose their jobs at the paper processing sites to apply to transfer and get the necessary training to work at IRS's phone centers.

- Census officials also reported that some employees will have different and additional responsibilities, such as a greater supervisory role, under the new management structure. They are developing training that they plan to implement in waves as the consolidation progresses.

We have previously reported that agencies may also expect to see higher rates of turnover following a consolidation because individuals do not see their place in the new organizations. As agency officials consider closing offices to reduce costs and streamline operations, they run the risk of losing their top performers located in affected offices. While some turnover is to be expected and is appropriate, the new organization must "re-recruit" its key talent to limit the loss of needed individuals. When re-recruiting key talent, top leaders should identify which competencies are

---

[55]GAO-12-317.

vital to the success of the new organization and select individuals who demonstrate those competencies.

- To minimize the risk of losing a considerable pool of talent and expertise all at once, Census officials told us that employees in the closing regional offices are being provided the opportunity to express interest in, and be considered for, existing vacancies elsewhere with the Census Bureau and Department of Commerce before any other internal or external recruitment actions are pursued.

Will the Implementation Plan Include a Strategy for Assessing and Mitigating Risk?

As we have demonstrated throughout this report, consolidations are inherently risky endeavors. There are up-front costs that can quickly spiral upward. Moreover, significant delays in the project timeline could negatively impact an agency's ability to carry out its core mission. To understand the various factors that could potentially derail a consolidation effort and make informed judgments concerning the actions needed to reduce those risks, we have previously described the importance and value of developing comprehensive plans for assessing and mitigating risks.[56] An effective implementation plan should identify all factors that will affect the program's cost, schedule, or technical status, including political, organizational, or business issues. Budget and funding risks, as well as risks associated with start-up activities, staffing, and organizational issues, should also be considered.

Identifying, analyzing, and developing ways to manage risks is a continuous process that leadership and managers should monitor on a regular and recurring basis throughout the consolidation.

- To help mitigate some of the major risks associated with consolidating the Human Resources Line of Business—such as selecting a provider agency that cannot adequately meet the needs of the client agency— OPM provided agencies with templates for conducting a risk analysis report and a fit gap analysis. The fit gap analysis template instructs customer agencies to perform a walk-through of each business process from beginning to end for each process scenario, show how the steps are supported by the provider agency, identify all shortcomings, and describe options for resolving those gaps. This resolution plan should provide an estimate of the implementation

---

[56]GAO, *Information Security Risk Assessment: Practices of Leading Organization,* GAO/AIMD-00-33 (Washington, D.C.: November, 1999).

effort including time and resources and be of sufficient detail to be used by other migration team members who are responsible for resolving the gap.

- Census officials developed a risk management plan intended to minimize the effect of unplanned events. Census created a Risk Review Board that meets monthly to assess and evaluate the effect of different categories of risks and to control changes to their master schedule. Some of the areas they are monitoring include the impact of the restructuring on affected employees, comprehension of new roles and responsibilities in the new operating environment, and security given the change in information technology architecture. Each identified risk is assigned a risk owner who must develop an analysis that includes a description of the risk, root cause, and possible impact on three major categories of the project: performance, cost, and schedule. The risk owner and review board will also determine the likelihood of occurrence on the basis of five categories ranging from extremely unlikely to extremely likely. Figure 2 has an identification form Census managers use to monitor risks. In addition to these planning and management steps, Census also added a 5 percent contingency to its restructuring budget to help absorb unforeseen costs.

GAO-12-542 Consolidation Proposals

Figure 2: Identification Form Census Managers Use to Monitor Risks

Risk Identification Form	
Risk Identification	
Risk Title:	
Risk Description:	
Root Cause:	
Impact Description:	
Timeframe of Risk:	
Risk Category:	
Risk Identified by:	
Name (Last name, first, name):	E-mail:
Phone :	Date:
Reference Information	
Project Team Name (if applicable):	
Risk Owner (Last name, first name):	Risk Monitor (Last name, first name):
Phone:	Phone:
E-mail:	E-mail:

Source: U.S. Census Bureau.

Is There a Strategy for Using the Consolidation Experiences of Other Organizations and Lessons Learned?

We have previously reported that managers of successful transformations seek to learn from best practices wherever they may be found.[57] Agency officials involved with consolidation efforts reported that they sought the advice of public and private sector managers about their consolidation experiences.

---

[57]GAO-03-239SP.

- For example, Census officials consulted with officials from Statistics Canada, Canada's national statistical agency, which had recently consolidated their operations. Specifically, Census officials were looking for advice on how to communicate internally and externally their decision to consolidate and what to expect in terms of employee reaction and morale. They also consulted with other federal statistical agencies as well as a variety of private, non-profit, and academic data collection organizations to better understand how these organizations manage field staff and provide them with secure access to sensitive programmatic and cost data. According to one Census official, the key lesson from these consultations was that consolidation is not only possible, but can lead to demonstrable gains in efficiency, at the same time that security can be maintained. He also reported that their counterparts advised that it is imperative to maintain constant communication at all levels and at every stage of the consolidation process.

- IRS and OPM officials reported that they implemented a lessons learned process after each phase of their consolidation plan to identify what worked well and what needed to be improved in future phases. According to IRS officials, after each site closure, they created a complete, searchable file of all documents related to the consolidation, and gave the next sites scheduled to close access. One official said that this repository of action plans, employee notifications, and other communications provided a blueprint for future consolidations and prevented unnecessary duplication of effort. OPM officials reported that post-implementation, each payroll provider agency met with representatives from the customer agencies to assess different aspects of the initiative such as project management and communication. OPM and the providers used that information to better plan and manage future migrations. According to OPM officials, the provider agencies were able to institute some changes on the basis of this feedback, such as involving both senior level managers and line personnel early in the planning stages and maintaining frequent communication including weekly conference calls and biweekly reviews of the project plan.

Agency Comments

We provided the draft for review and comment to the five agencies with consolidation initiatives that were not covered by prior GAO work and made technical changes as appropriate.

We are sending copies of this report to the appropriate congressional committees and other interested parties. The report is also available at no charge on the GAO website at http://www.gao.gov. If you have any questions concerning this report, please contact me at (202) 512-6806 or mihmj@gao.gov. Contact points for our Offices of Congressional Relations and Public Affairs may be found on the last page of this report. Key contributors to this report are listed in appendix IV.

J. Christopher Mihm
Managing Director, Strategic Issues

Appendix I: Scope and Methodology

To identify key questions that federal agencies should consider when evaluating whether to consolidate physical infrastructure or management functions, we identified and reviewed relevant literature on public sector consolidations produced by academic institutions, professional associations, think tanks, news outlets, and various other organizations. This information complemented our review of GAO's extensive body of work on government reform. Specifically, we reviewed close to 50 reports produced from 1980 to 2011 that recommended or commented on consolidation of physical infrastructure or management functions at the federal level.

We interviewed practitioners and academic experts in public management and government reform including Jitinder Kohli from the Center for American Progress; John Koskinen from Freddie Mac; Rosemary O'Leary from the Maxwell School of Syracuse University; and Paul Posner from the School of Public and International Affairs, George Mason University. We also interviewed former officials from the Office of Management and Budget; Karen Evans, Mark Forman, John Marshall, and Robert Shea, knowledgeable about management function consolidations and the Lines of Business initiative. We selected these practitioners and experts on the basis of our literature review and recommendations from other experts. We also met with a panel of Fellows from the National Academy of Public Administration, comprising former government executives.[1] Participants included Jonathan Breul; Doris Hausser; Dwight Ink; Susan Jacobs; Herbert Jasper; John Kamensky; Albert Kliman; F. Stevens Redburn; and Thomas Stanton. The participants described their consolidation experiences at federal agencies such as the Office of Management and Budget; the Office of Personnel Management; the U.S. Agency for International Development; the U.S. Department of Agriculture; the Department of Health and Human Services; and the Department of Housing and Urban Development.

Using our literature review and interviews, we derived a set of questions to help decision makers evaluate whether consolidation of physical infrastructure or management functions will lead to greater efficiencies or effectiveness. We provided the questions to many of the individuals we

---

[1]Established in 1967 and chartered by Congress, the National Academy of Public Administration is a non-profit, independent coalition of public management and organizational leaders. For more information, go to www.napawash.org.

interviewed for their review and incorporated their comments where appropriate.

To illustrate how agencies have attempted to address the questions about consolidation, we selected eight consolidation examples at the federal agency level. These examples include a mix of physical infrastructure and management functions, intra-agency and interagency initiatives, and recommended, ongoing, and completed efforts. For our illustrative examples, we reviewed documentation such as cost analyses and performance plans to obtain information about how agencies planned and implemented consolidation efforts and collected through interviews and document requests information from the agencies on how they estimated, gathered, or calculated consolidation cost savings. Because it was not the purpose of this report to assess the anticipated or actual success of consolidation efforts, we did not attempt to independently verify the reliability of these data or estimates. As a result, the reported estimated or actual cost savings are of undetermined reliability. We also conducted interviews with agency officials responsible for implementing the consolidation initiatives, as well as union representatives from the National Treasury Employees Union. In the examples of the Department of Defense's Base Realignment and Closure, the Environmental Protection Agency's laboratories, the Office of Management and Budget's data center consolidation, and the Department of State's International Cooperative Administration Support Services, we relied on our recently published reports.[2] Table 4 lists the consolidation initiatives and the types of consolidation for the examples we included in the report.

[2]We drew from our prior reports: GAO, *Military Base Realignments and Closures: Key Factors Contributing to BRAC 2005 Results,* GAO-12-513T (Washington, D.C.: Mar. 8, 2012); *Military Base Realignments and Closures: Estimated Costs Have Increased While Savings Estimates Have Decreased Since Fiscal Year 2009,* GAO-10-98R (Washington D.C.: Nov. 13, 2009); *Military Bases: Analysis of DOD's 2005 Selection Process and Recommendations for Base Closures and Realignments,* GAO-05-785 (Washington, D.C.: July 1, 2005); *Environmental Protection Agency: To Better Fulfill Its Mission, EPA Needs a More Coordinated Approach to Managing its Laboratories,* GAO-11-347 (Washington, D.C.: July 25, 2011); *Data Center Consolidation: Agencies Need to Complete Inventories and Plans to Achieve Expected Savings,* GAO-11-565 (Washington, D.C.: July 19, 2011); and *Embassy Management: State Department and Other Agencies Should Further Explore Opportunities to Save Administrative Costs Overseas,* GAO-12-317 (Washington, D.C.: Jan. 31, 2012).

Table 4: Federal Agency Consolidation Examples in Various Stages of Implementation

Consolidation initiative	Type of consolidation
Department of Commerce Census Bureau Regional Offices	Intra-agency / physical infrastructure
Department of Defense Base Realignment and Closure	Intra-agency / physical infrastructure
Department of the Treasury Internal Revenue Service Processing Centers	Intra-agency / physical infrastructure
Environmental Protection Agency Laboratories	Recommended intra-agency / physical infrastructure
Office of Management and Budget Federal Data Center Consolidation Initiative	Intra-agency / physical infrastructure and management function
Office of Personnel Management Payroll Systems	Interagency / management function
Department of State International Cooperative Administrative Support Services System	Interagency / management function
Department of Veterans Affairs and Department of Defense Federal Health Care Center	Interagency / physical infrastructure and management function

Source: GAO.

We did not attempt to identify all consolidation efforts of physical infrastructure and management functions at the federal level that could have illustrated the questions, challenges, and practices that decision makers could adopt to help them overcome challenges. While we believe that these questions, challenges, and practices are applicable across different agencies and for various types of consolidation efforts, with our approach we are not able to definitively say that the experiences associated with these consolidation activities can be applied successfully to future federal consolidation initiatives.

We provided the draft for review and comment to the five agencies with consolidation initiatives that were not covered by prior GAO work and made technical changes as appropriate. We conducted our work from June 2011 to May 2012 in the Washington, D.C., metropolitan area in accordance with all sections of GAO's Quality Assurance Framework that are relevant to our objective. The framework requires that we plan and perform the engagement to obtain sufficient and appropriate evidence to meet our stated objectives and to discuss any limitations in our work. We believe that the information and data obtained, and the analysis conducted, provide a reasonable basis for any findings and conclusions in this product.

Appendix II: Additional Questions Related to Physical Infrastructure and Management Function Consolidation Initiatives

The following are additional sub-questions related to the ideas, strategies, and leading practices that may facilitate physical infrastructure or management function consolidations. This list is not exhaustive, nor is it necessary for an agency to consider every listed question. Rather, the presence of some of these considerations may indicate that agency officials have developed a sound consolidation strategy. Conversely, the absence of consideration of these questions could indicate that agency officials have not adequately planned their physical infrastructure or management function consolidation.

What Are the Goals of the Consolidation? What Opportunities Will Be Addressed through the Consolidation and What Problems Will Be Solved? What Problems, If Any, Will Be Created?

- Have agency leaders identified specific goals to be achieved through consolidation?
- Have agency leaders assessed how consolidation can help an agency incorporate changes in technology, business processes, or the needs of customers or clients?
- How have agency leaders weighed the importance of achieving the goals against a realistic assessment of the effort that will be required to achieve them?
- How have agency leaders considered the risks to consolidation that could prevent the achievement of goals and planned for ways to manage them?
- Are agency leaders defining the benefits associated with consolidation and describing how the future will be both different from and better than the past?
- Are agency leaders providing a clear and compelling picture of what will constitute success?

What Will Be the Likely Costs and Benefits of the Consolidation? Are Sufficiently Reliable Data Available to Support a Business-Case Analysis or Cost-Benefit Analysis?

- What data on the likely costs and benefits of a consolidation are available?
- Are the data sufficiently accurate and reliable? What data on the likely costs and benefits of a consolidation are unavailable, and has a plan been developed to mitigate the unavailability or unreliability of certain data?
- On the basis of the data available, can a reasonable expectation of a consolidation's costs and benefits be drawn?

- Have the likely costs and benefits been subjected to a sensitivity analysis? How sensitive are the estimated costs and benefits to variation in less reliable data or other key assumptions?

How Can the Up-Front Costs Associated with the Consolidation Be Funded?

- Can immediate efficiencies or uncommitted funds in other areas be redirected to pay for the up-front costs of a consolidation?
- Has the agency considered how it will assess return on investment for any funding for up-front costs?
- Can a working capital fund or other funds be drawn on as a funding mechanism?
- Is Congress amenable to establishing a funding mechanism for a consolidation and appropriating funds for it?

Who are the Consolidation Stakeholders, and How Will They Be Affected? How Have the Stakeholders Been Involved in the Decision, and How Have their Views Been Considered? On Balance, Do Stakeholders Understand the Rationale for Consolidation?

- Have agency leaders identified affected stakeholders?
- Have agency leaders determined the necessary frequency and timing of communication about the consolidation to internal and external stakeholders?
- Does the communication strategy allow for a two-way exchange of information between management and stakeholders?
- How is the agency planning to involve employees to obtain their ideas and get their support? Have union representatives been consulted? Are there employee task teams responsible for developing and proposing common solutions to particular issues related to the consolidation?
- How does the agency plan to provide information to employees about how their jobs might be affected, what their rights and protections might be, or how their responsibilities might change with the new organization?
- Is the agency planning to communicate information through different channels such as e-mail, face-to-face meetings, large and small group meetings, intranet websites, and town hall meetings?

To What Extent Do Plans Show That Change Management Practices Will Be Used to Implement the Consolidation?

Will Top Leadership Be Engaged in Driving the Consolidation Plan?

- Do agency leaders have plans to move deliberately to demonstrate their conviction and commitment to making the needed changes?
- Do agency leaders have plans to provide clear guidance to employees about how to conduct business during a potentially turbulent period?

Will a Dedicated Implementation Team Lead the Consolidation?

- Will the implementation team have strong program management skills and a proven record of successfully working through or overseeing major transformations?
- Are there networks such as senior executive councils, functional teams, or cross-cutting teams that can ensure that changes are thoroughly implemented and sustained over time?

Will the Implementation Plan Include Metrics to Measure Progress toward the Consolidation's Goals?

- Will there be an action plan with goals and milestones to track progress and identify any needed mid-course adjustments?
- Will an action plan identify critical phases and the essential activities that need to be completed by and on any given date? Are there plans to publicize and report progress on specific goals for each phase of the initiative?
- Is there a strategy for tracking employee attitudes toward the consolidation and identifying any morale or productivity issues?
- Will the implementation plan include a strategy for attracting and retaining key talent?

Will the Implementation Plan Include a Strategy for Assessing and Mitigating Risk?

- Will the implementation plan be informed by a risk assessment that includes the following five steps?

  - Set strategic goals and objectives, and determine constraints
  - Assess risks
  - Evaluate alternatives for addressing these risks
  - Select the appropriate alternatives
  - Implement the alternatives and monitor progress made and results achieved

Is there a Strategy for Using the Consolidation Experiences of Other Organizations and Lessons Learned?

- Have agency officials involved with the consolidation initiative identified and consulted with other agencies or organizations that planned for or implemented a similar consolidation effort?
- Is there a process for capturing lessons learned after each phase of the consolidation and using the information to improve the management of subsequent phases?

Appendix III: Key Change Management Practices

Highlights

Highlights of GAO-03-293SP

November 2002

HIGHLIGHTS OF A GAO FORUM

Mergers and Transformation: Lessons Learned for a Department of Homeland Security and Other Federal Agencies

Why GAO Convened This Forum

The early years of the 21ˢᵗ century are proving to be a period of profound transition for our world, our country, and our government. The federal government needs to engage in a comprehensive review, reassessment, reprioritization, and as appropriate, re-engineering of what the government does, how it does business, and in some cases, who does the government's business. Leading public and private organizations in the United States and abroad have found that for organizations to successfully transform themselves they must often fundamentally change their culture.

On September 24, 2002, GAO convened a forum to identify and discuss useful practices and lessons learned from major private and public sector organizational mergers, acquisitions, and transformations that federal agencies could implement to successfully transform their cultures and a new Department of Homeland Security could use to merge its various originating components into a unified department. The invited participants have experience managing or studying large-scale organizational mergers, acquisitions, and transformations.

What Participants Said

There are a number of key practices that have consistently been found at the center of successful mergers, acquisitions, and transformations and can serve as a basis for subsequent consideration as federal agencies seek to transform their cultures in response to governance challenges. These practices include the following.

1. **Ensure top leadership drives the transformation.** Leadership must set the direction, pace, and tone and provide a clear, consistent rationale that brings everyone together behind a single mission.

2. **Establish a coherent mission and integrated strategic goals to guide the transformation.** Together the mission and goals define the culture and serve as a vehicle for employees to unite and rally around.

3. **Focus on a key set of principles and priorities at the outset of the transformation.** A clear set of principles and priorities serve as a framework to help the organization create a new culture and drive employee behaviors.

4. **Set implementation goals and a timeline to build momentum and show progress from day one.** Goals and a timeline are essential because the transformation could take years to complete.

5. **Dedicate an implementation team to manage the transformation process.** A strong and stable team is important to ensure that the transformation receives the needed attention to be sustained and successful.

6. **Use the performance management system to define responsibility and assure accountability for change.** A "line of sight" shows how team, unit, and individual performance can contribute to overall organizational results.

7. **Establish a communication strategy to create shared expectations and report related progress.** The strategy must reach out to employees, customers, and stakeholders and engage them in a two-way exchange.

8. **Involve employees to obtain their ideas and gain their ownership for the transformation.** Employee involvement strengthens the process and allows them to share their experiences and shape policies.

9. **Build a world-class organization.** Building on a vision of improved performance, the organization adopts the most efficient, effective, and economical personnel, system, and process changes and continually seeks to implement best practices.

www.gao.gov/cgi-bin/getrpt? GAO-03-293SP.

To view the full report, including the scope and methodology, click on the link above. For more information, contact J. Christopher Mihm at (202) 512-6806 or mihmj@gao.gov.

_____ United States General Accounting Office

Highlights

Highlights of GAO-03-669, a report to
congressional requesters

July 2003

RESULTS-ORIENTED CULTURES

Implementation Steps to Assist Mergers and Organizational Transformations

Why GAO Did This Study

The Comptroller General convened a forum in September 2002 to identify useful practices and lessons learned from major private and public sector mergers, acquisitions, and organizational transformations. This was done to help federal agencies implement successful transformations of their cultures, as well as the new Department of Homeland Security merge its various originating components into a unified department. There was general agreement on a number of key practices found at the center of successful mergers, acquisitions, and transformations. In this report, we identify the specific implementation steps for the key practices raised at the forum with illustrative private and public sector examples.

To identify these implementation steps and examples, we relied primarily on interviews with selected forum participants and other experts about their experiences implementing mergers, acquisitions, and transformations and also conducted a literature review.

www.gao.gov/cgi-bin/getrpt?GAO-03-669.

To view the full product, including the scope and methodology, click on the link above. For more information, contact J. Christopher Mihm, (202) 512-6806 or mihmj@gao.gov.

What GAO Found

At the center of any serious change management initiative are the people. Thus, the key to a successful merger and transformation is to recognize the "people" element and implement strategies to help individuals maximize their full potential in the new organization, while simultaneously managing the risk of reduced productivity and effectiveness that often occurs as a result of the changes. Building on the lessons learned from the experiences of large private and public sector organizations, these key practices and implementation steps can help agencies transform their cultures so that they can be more results oriented, customer focused, and collaborative in nature.

Key Practices and Implementation Steps for Mergers and Organizational Transformations

Practice	Implementation Step
Ensure top leadership drives the transformation.	• Define and articulate a succinct and compelling reason for change. • Balance continued delivery of services with merger and transformation activities.
Establish a coherent mission and integrated strategic goals to guide the transformation.	• Adopt leading practices for results-oriented strategic planning and reporting.
Focus on a key set of principles and priorities at the outset of the transformation.	• Embed core values in every aspect of the organization to reinforce the new culture.
Set implementation goals and a timeline to build momentum and show progress from day one.	• Make public implementation goals and timeline. • Seek and monitor employee attitudes and take appropriate follow-up actions. • Identify cultural features of merging organizations to increase understanding of former work environments. • Attract and retain key talent. • Establish an organizationwide knowledge and skills inventory to exchange knowledge among merging organizations.
Dedicate an implementation team to manage the transformation process.	• Establish networks to support implementation team. • Select high-performing team members.
Use the performance management system to define responsibility and assure accountability for change.	• Adopt leading practices to implement effective performance management systems with adequate safeguards.
Establish a communication strategy to create shared expectations and report related progress.	• Communicate early and often to build trust. • Ensure consistency of message. • Encourage two-way communication. • Provide information to meet specific needs of employees.
Involve employees to obtain their ideas and gain their ownership for the transformation.	• Use employee teams. • Involve employees in planning and sharing performance information. • Incorporate employee feedback into new policies and procedures. • Delegate authority to appropriate organizational levels.
Build a world-class organization.	• Adopt leading practices to build a world-class organization.

Source: GAO.

_____ United States General Accounting Office

Appendix IV: GAO Contact and Staff Acknowledgments

GAO Contact	J. Christopher Mihm, (202) 512-6806 or mihmj@gao.gov
Staff Acknowledgments	In addition to the contact named above, Elizabeth Curda, Assistant Director, and Judith Kordahl, Analyst-in-Charge, supervised the development of this report. Jessica Nierenberg and Dan Webb made significant contributions to all aspects of this report. Martin De Alteriis assisted with the design and methodology. A.J. Stephens provided legal counsel. Janice Latimer and Kathleen Padulchick verified the information in the report, and Donna Miller developed the report's graphics.

Other important contributors included Vijaykumar Barnabas; Jill Center; Carol Henn; David Hinchman; Diane LoFaro; James Michels; Angela Miles; Susan Offutt; Joanna Stamatiades; and Laura Talbott. |